IRON MAN 2

INSIDE...

SECRET MISSION...

Warning! An unknown agent has infiltrated Stark Industries with a swarm of **Mini-Drones**. I need your help to track them down, so keep your eyes open as you look through the annual.

Each drone has a letter on its spy-tail.

Once you've found all **9** rearrange them to reveal the name of the culprit. Good Luck!

...MAN 2 ANNUAL 2011 is published by Panini Publishing, a division of Panini UK Limited. Editorial: Ed Hammond, Design: Alex Foot. Office of publication: Brockbourne, ...77 Mount Ephraim, Tunbridge Wells, Kent TN4 8BS. MARVEL, Iron Man and all related characters: TM & Copyright © 2010 Marvel Entertainment, LLC and its sub-...es. Iron Man 2, the Movie © 2010 MVL Film Finance LLC. Marvel, Iron Man, all character names and their distinctive likenesses: TM & © 2010 Marvel Entertainment, ...d its subsidiaries. All Rights Reserved. No similarity between any of the names, characters, persons and/or institutions in this annual with any living or dead person ...ons intended, and any similarity which may exist is purely coincidental. This publication may not be sold except by authorised dealers and is sold subject to the ...tution is intended, and any similarity which may exist is purely coincidental. This publication may not be sold except by authorised dealers and is sold subject to the ...tions that it shall not be sold or distributed with any part of its cover or markings removed, nor in a mutilated condition. Printed in Italy. ISBN: 978-1-84653-110-1

STARK 7

£7.99

LOCATING FILE... ACCESS CODE: *YINSEN1*

TONY STARK/IRON MAN

FILE UNLOCKED... ACCESS GRANTED...

ORIGINS

STARK

Billionaire businessman Tony Stark was the head of Stark Industries, one of the world's largest weapons manufacturers. Whilst demonstrating the new 'Jericho' Missile system, he was captured by a terrorist group called the Ten Rings.

ARC AID

Gravely injured in the attack, Stark desperately needed medical attention to remove pieces of **shrapnel** lodged perilously close to his heart. With the help of another prisoner, Professor Yinsen, Stark was able to build a **miniature ARC reactor**, which he attached to his chest. Acting like a magnet, the reactor stopped the pieces of metal from entering his heart.

IRON ULTIMATUM

Stark's captors gave him an ultimatum. Build them a Jericho missile system or face **execution**. Instead, he secretly began building a mechanised suit of armour, powered by the ARC reactor. Once finished, he used his new armour to bust out of his prison and escape his captors.

A NEW VISION

Tony Stark returned to America a changed man. He had seen first hand the **devastation** caused by his weapons and decreed that Stark Industries would no longer build military equipment.

UPGRADES

Unknown to those around him, he also began working on a **new armoured suit**. Tony redesigned his original plans, making the suit sleeker, more agile and much more powerful. He became the invincible **Iron Man**.

ARMOURED AVENGER

Since then, Tony Stark has used the power of his incredible Iron Man armour to become a great force for good in the world, risking his life time after time to save countless innocent lives.

DESTRUCTIVE RE-ENTRY!

Heads up, people. Someone is causing a big mess onboard the Stark close orbit lab station Delphi 1. JARVIS has pulled up a file on the most likely candidate, so check it out whilst I prep the Iron Man suit for zero G...

>>JARVIS ONLINE
>>REFINING SEARCH>>> 10% 50% 75% 100%>>>>
>>>>MOST LIKELY CULPRIT>>>>>

THE LIVING LASER!

Real Name: Arthur Parks

Powers and Abilities: Photonic body, light manipulation, laser projection, hologram creation and invisibility.

Whilst researching an experimental process to turn matter into pure energy, physicist Arthur Parks accidentally transformed his own body into one made of pure light.

Desperate to regain his physical form, Parks is prepared to do anything in his power to become fully human once again.

DELPHI-1 RESEARCH STATION

Specialist outer space laboratory positioned in geo-synchronous orbit with Earth. Primarily used for cutting edge future science research into nano-technology.

NANO-ROBOTS

Microscopic programmable machines capable of building matter at a cellular level.

FRED VAN LENTE   JAMES CORDEIRO   GARY ERSKINE   MARTEGOD GRACIA   DAVE SHARPE
WRITER   PENCILER   INKER   COLORIST   LETTERER
SKOTTIE YOUNG   ANTHONY DIAL   NATHAN COSBY   MARK PANICCIA   JOE QUESADA   DAN BUCKLEY
COVER   PRODUCTION   ASST. EDITOR   EDITOR   EDITOR IN CHIEF   PUBLISHER

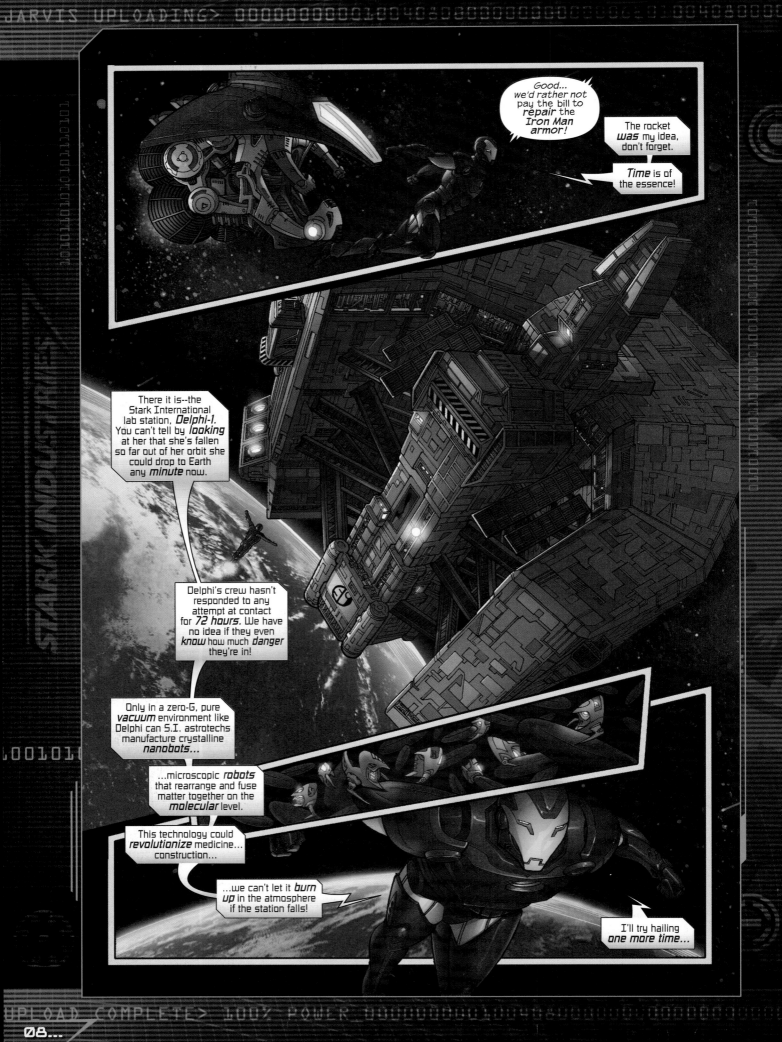

Good... we'd rather not pay the bill to *repair* the *Iron Man* armor!

The rocket *was* my idea, don't forget.

Time is of the essence!

There it is--the Stark International lab station, *Delphi-1*. You can't tell by *looking* at her that she's fallen so far out of her orbit she could drop to Earth any *minute* now.

Delphi's crew hasn't responded to any attempt at contact for *72 hours*. We have no idea if they even *know* how much *danger* they're in!

Only in a zero-G, pure *vacuum* environment like Delphi can S.I. astrotechs manufacture crystalline *nanobots*...

...microscopic *robots* that rearrange and fuse matter together on the *molecular* level.

This technology could *revolutionize* medicine... construction...

...we can't let it *burn up* in the atmosphere if the station falls!

I'll try hailing *one more time*...

Nothing.

Guess there's no point in *knocking.*

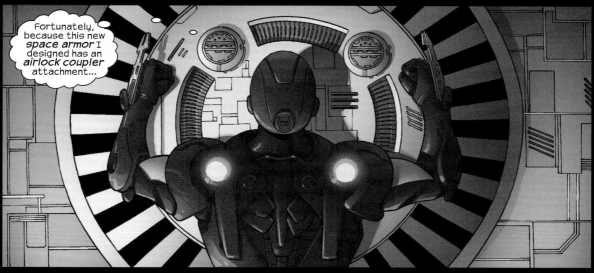

Fortunately, because this new *space armor* I designed has an *airlock coupler* attachment...

CLICK

VRRRRR

...I can let *myself* in.

Hello?

Anybody *home...?*

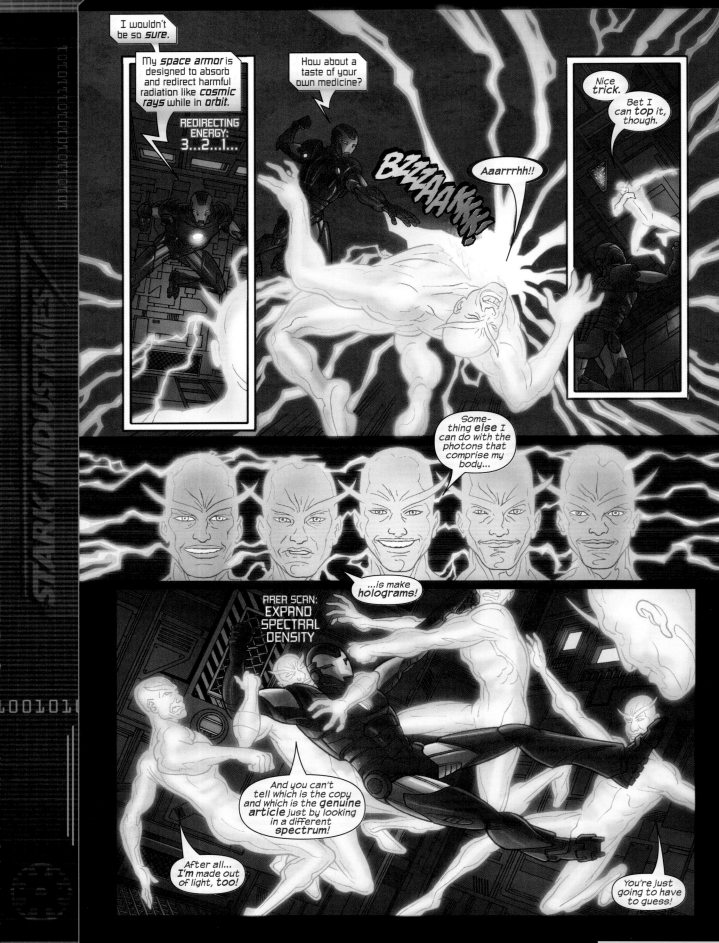

CONTINUED ON PAGE 16...

MK IV ARMOUR

LOCATING FILE...
ACCESS CODE: TS390363

IRON MAN
MK IV ARMOUR

FILE UNLOCKED...
ACCESS GRANTED...

Each eye piece has an advanced heads-up display, featuring critical combat and internal system information.

Outer armour constructed from a light weight, but super strong Titanium Alloy.

ARC REACTOR
ENERGY OUTPUT:
8 GIGAJOULES PER SECOND

WARNING!
RECENTLY, TONY STARK HAS DISCOVERED THAT HE IS BEING SLOWLY POISONED BY THE PALLADIUM LEAKING FROM HIS ARC REACTOR. HIS ONLY HOPE IS TO FIND A MORE STABLE CHEMICAL COMPOUND TO REPLACE IT, BEFORE HIS BODY IS DAMAGED BEYOND REPAIR.

The palm of each hand features a powerful Repulsor Ray that fires a super-charged particle beam capable of disintegrating most metals.

Electronic exo-skeleton allows Tony Stark to lift up to 3 tons.

Jet thrusters in boots can propel the suit to more than 1,500 miles per hour, easily breaking the sound barrier.

WHIPLASH

PAST CRIMES

Anton Vanko was a Russian scientist who helped Tony Stark's father, Howard Stark, build the very first **ARC reactor**. However, Anton was deported to Siberia when Stark discovered that he was trying to sell the technology to another company.

FAMILY SECRETS

Years later, whilst on his deathbed, Anton told his son Ivan the truth behind the ARC reactor. Ivan was convinced that Howard Stark had **stolen** the reactor technology from his father and began to plot his **revenge**.

The original ARC reactor at Stark Industries.

ULTIMATE POWER

Following his father's blueprints, Ivan created a miniature ARC reactor, which he used to fuel two **electrical whips**. With his energized appendages, he now had the power to get his revenge on **Stark Industries**, starting with Howard Stark's son Tony.

LIGHTNING STRIKE

Ivan used his Whiplash armour to attack Tony Stark whilst he was taking part in a car race. Crashing on to the track he launched a **flurry of blows** at him, slicing his vehicle to ribbons. Tony quickly donned his Iron Man armour and, after a hard fought battle, managed to subdue Ivan.

STARK VICTORY

Even though Whiplash had been stopped, Iron Man's armour had been severely compromised. As Vanko had planned, this defeat planted **seeds of doubt** in the watching world – it now seemed that Iron Man wasn't invincible after all...

IVAN VANKO / WHIPLASH

FILE UNLOCKED... ACCESS GRANTED...

SUPER STRENGTH

Hydraulic arm and leg attachments increase Whiplash's strength by roughly three times.

ENERGY WHIPS

Unlike Iron Man, Whiplash has found a very different way of utilizing the excess energy from his ARC reactor. Instead of focusing it into repulsor rays, Whiplash transmits the energy through ionized plasma channels to his whips – turning them into lethal razor sharp weapons that can cut through any metal!

CYBER CRIMINAL

Along with being a highly skilled electronics engineer, Ivan is also an expert computer hacker.

Quite the contrary. I'm **gaining** a body.

An exact **replica** of the one I lost because of **you!**

It's only fitting your nanobots **build** it for me.

"It was merciless competition from **Stark International** that pushed **my** company--Parks Industries--to the brink of **bankruptcy!**"

"If it weren't for **you,** I never would have cut so many **corners** in my pursuit of physics' Holy Grail...

"...a means to convert **matter** to energy!"

It's **your** fault I was transformed into this photosynthetic **horror**-- a **ghost** made out of **light!**

But soon I'll be **human** again-- able to return to my wife and daughter--

--once I **download** my consciousness into my new **synthetic** body!

I transferred my brainwave patterns into the Delphi mainframe in the form of **electrons**--

SSHHHRAAKKK!

You mean **this** mainframe, here?

NOOOOOOO!

The download had already **begun!** I've got to stop the **data** stream before any particles are **lost**--

Did it ever occur to you to just *ask* for help?

Oh, and remain beholden to my greatest *enemy* for the rest of my life?

Don't make me *laugh!*

I can only count on *my-self* for a cure...

...after I destroy *you*-- for all you've *done* to me!

DETECTING: 2 ENTITIES

Scanning...
1st entity: composed of: photons
%%error%% cannot reassemble
Is that... the remains of my nanobot body?
2nd entity: composed of:
Flexi-iron shell--organic interior
Reassembling: initiated
The nanobots are attacking the molecules in my glove--
--reassembling them into more nanobots!

ARMOUR ART!

Listen up, Shellheads. Think you could be a Stark Industries engineer? Grab your pens and pencils and practice your skills on the two battlesuits below!

WAR MACHINE

IRON MAN

...CONTINUED FROM PAGE 21

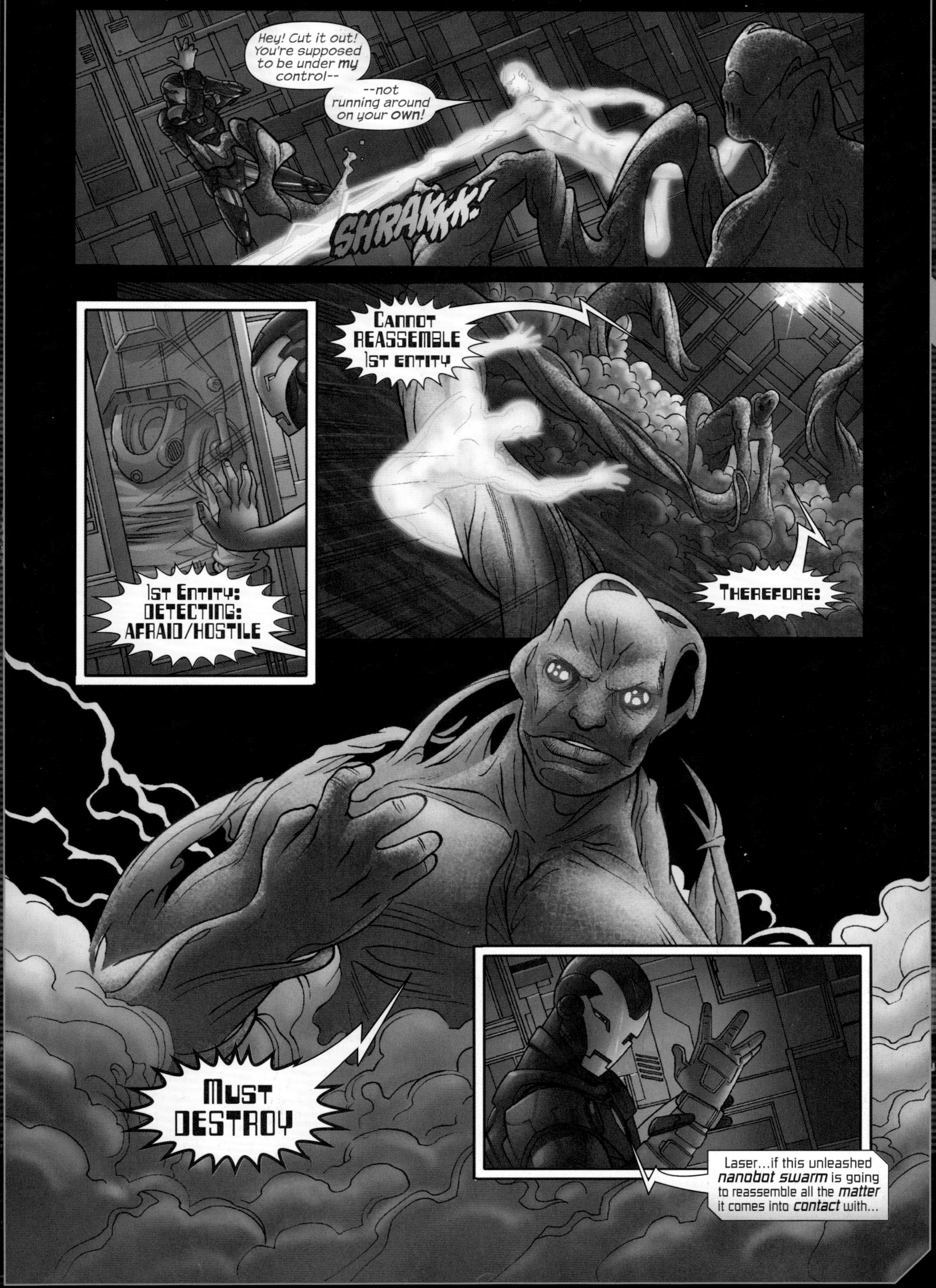

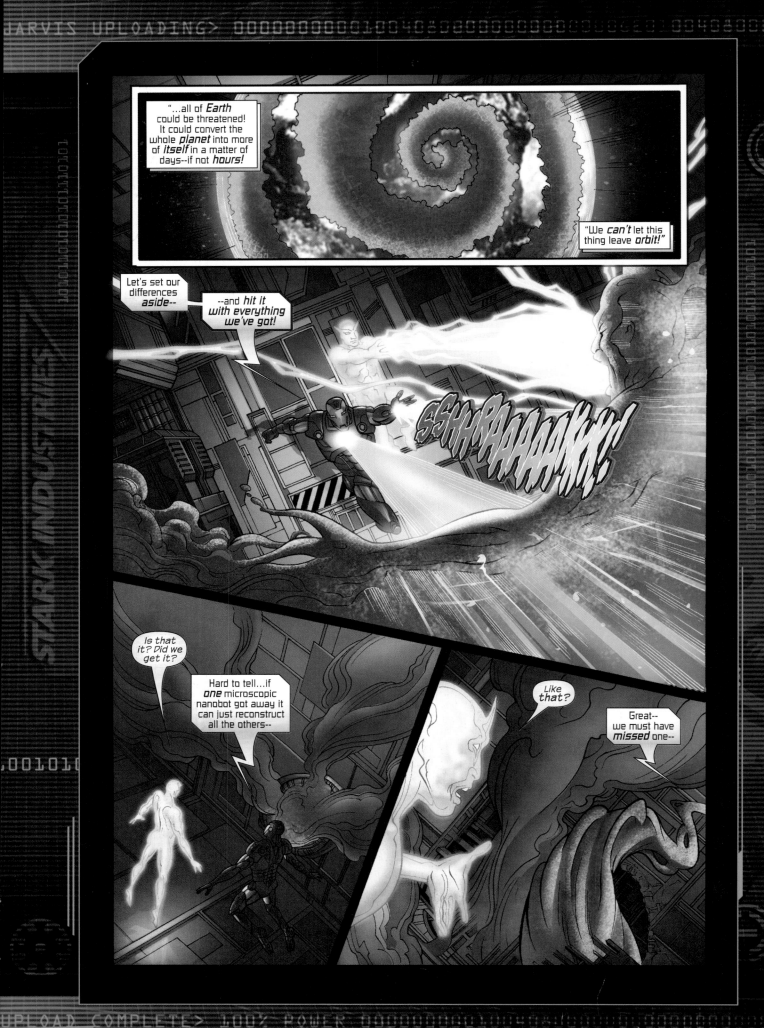

JARVIS UPLOADING>

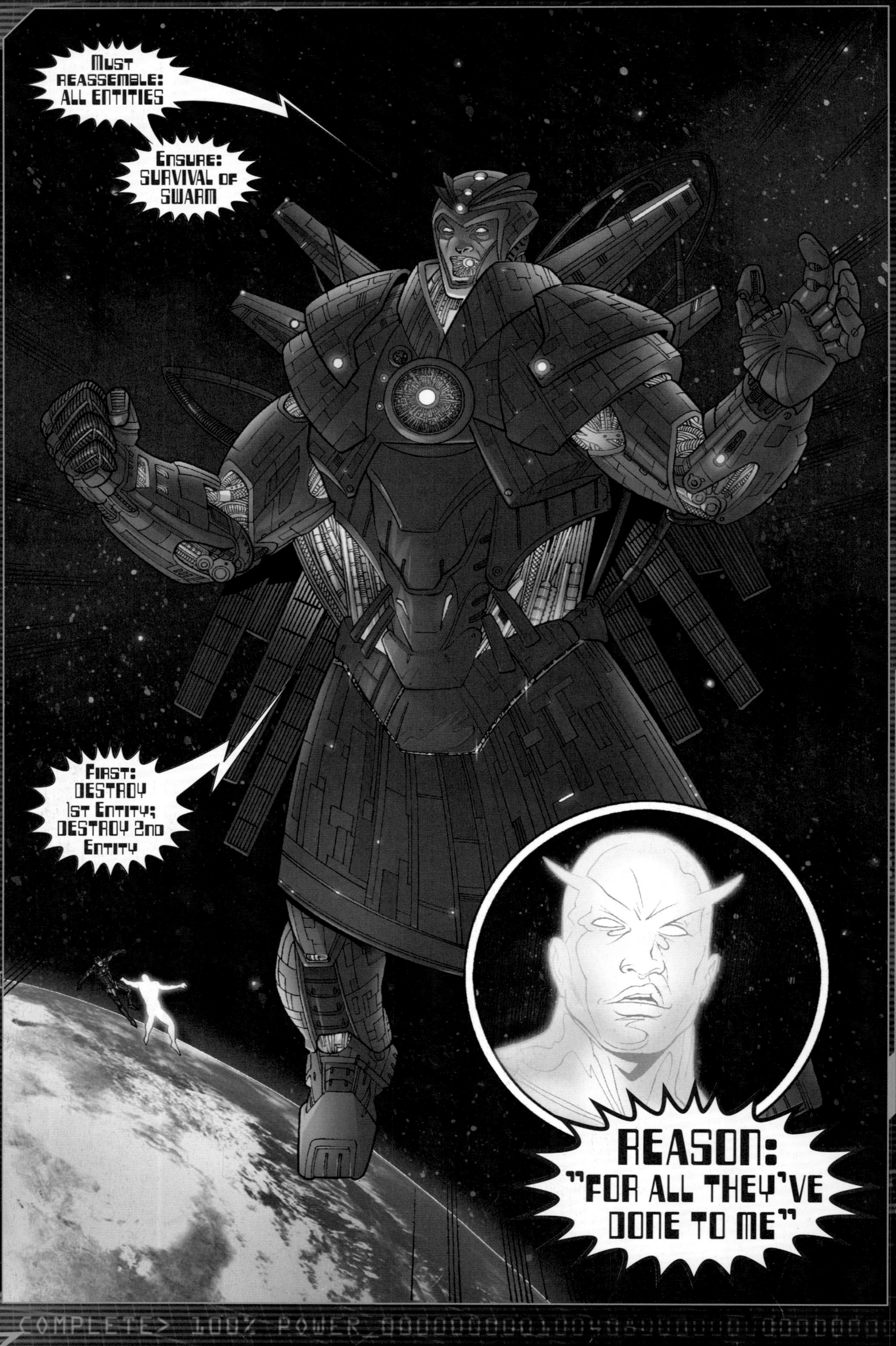

UPLOAD COMPLETE> 100% POWER

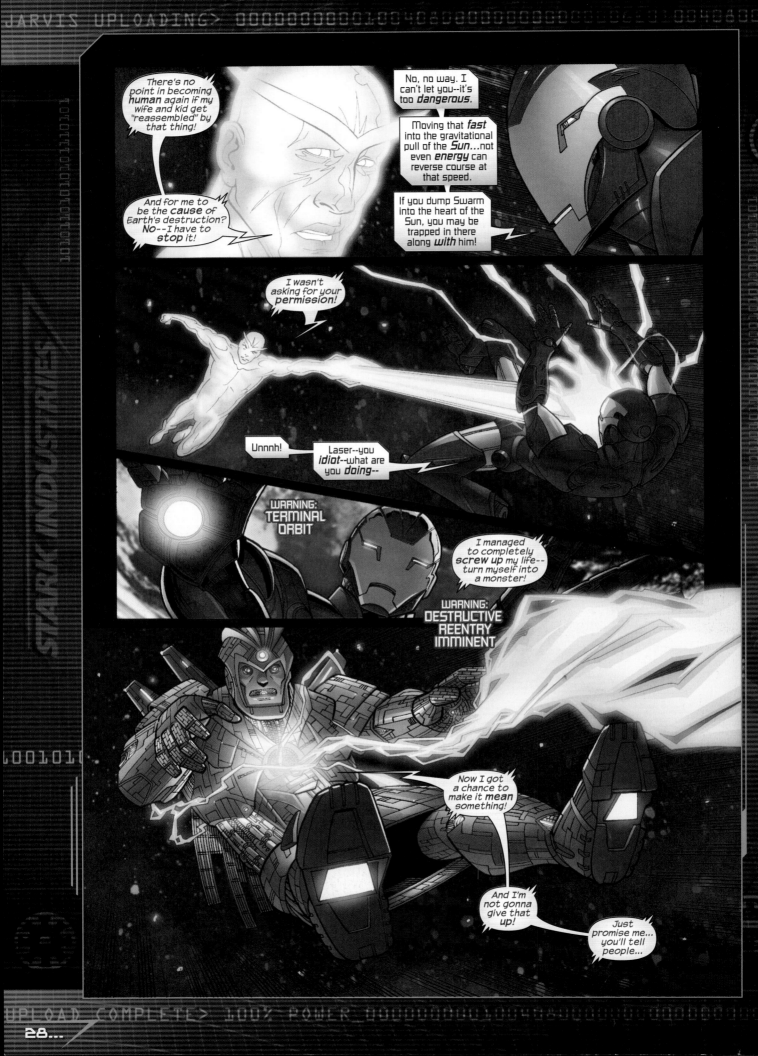

BLACK WIDOW

MYSTERIOUS GIRL

Following her promotion to CEO of Stark Industries, Pepper Potts appointed a young Notary Public called Natasha Rushman to be Tony Stark's new **Personal Assistant**.

Tony was immediately captivated by his beautiful, highly organized and quick thinking new assistant. Little did he realise though, that there was more to Natasha than **met the eye**... She was in fact Agent Romanoff AKA the Black Widow – S.H.I.E.L.D.'s number one espionage agent.

SPY GAMES

Discovering that Tony was being slowly poisoned by the **palladium** in his miniature ARC reactor, S.H.I.E.L.D. sent the Black Widow to infiltrate Stark Industries. Her mission was to keep tabs on Tony Stark and monitor his health. It is up to the Black Widow to protect Tony and stop the Iron Man armour's secrets from falling into the wrong hands.

S.H.I.E.L.D. REVEALED!

The Strategic Homeland Intervention, Enforcement and Logistics Division (S.H.I.E.L.D.) is an ultra-top secret organisation that control all matters of international security. Ever since Tony Stark first created the Iron Man suit, S.H.I.E.L.D.'s Director Col. Nick Fury has kept his eye on him. It seems that Fury may need Iron Man's help for an ultra-secret project codenamed the Avengers Initiative. But who or what that could be remains to be seen.

NATASHA ROMANOFF/ BLACK WIDOW

WARNING! FOR S.H.I.E.L.D. EYES ONLY.

Her belt contains a selection of miniature smoke, high explosive and stun grenades.

The Black Widow possesses Olympic-level gymnastic and athletic skills.

She has an extensive knowledge of martial arts, including karate, judo, aikido, kung fu and street boxing.

Each of her bracelets is able to fire a short energy blast, known as her 'Widow's Sting', along with a thin line and grappling hook.

THE CREEPING DOOM!

Since giving up the weapons game, Stark Industries is all about saving the planet, rather than trying to blow it to smithereens!

One of our bioresearch scientists in Mexico has made an amazing breakthrough that could revolutionise crop growing. So check out the Personnel File below, and then we'll head out as soon as Rhodey finishes refuelling the jet...

FILE 00-891
SAMUEL SMITHERS

One of the World's leading botanist and bio-engineers, Samuel Smithers is a reclusive scientist who seems to prefer the company of plants to that of other people.

His last known location was Dusty Gulch, New Mexico. However, no one has heard from him since he submitted his research work to Stark Industries a few months ago.

WARNING! OXYGEN LEVELS DANGEROUSLY LOW!

BREATHABLE AIR RESERVES AT 1.35% CAPACITY AND DROPPING! WARNING!

WHERE...

WHERE AM I...?

THE CREEPING DOOM

Fred Van Lente - Writer   Ronan Cliquet - Penciler   Amilton Santos - Inker   Studio F's Martegod Gracia - Colorist
Blambot's Nate Piekos - Letterer   Michael Golden - Cover Artist   Brad Johansen - Production
Nathan Cosby - Assistant Editor   Mark Paniccia - Editor   Joe Quesada - Editor in Chief   Dan Buckley - Publisher

ARMOUR UP!

ARMS RACE!

To effectively pilot the Iron Man armour you need to think one step ahead of your enemies at all times. Prove you can do this by navigating the test course, without running into any of the military drones.

START!

FINISH!

MULTIPLE MENACE!

Only one of these pictures of Whiplash is an exact match to the original. Can you spot which one it is?

ORIGINAL

EVEN WITH THE HELP OF JARVIS, CONTROLLING THE IRON MAN SUIT AT NEAR SUPERSONIC SPEEDS REQUIRES TONY STARK TO HAVE AMAZING OBSERVATION SKILLS.

SEE IF YOU TOO HAVE GOT WHAT IT TAKES BY BEATING THESE TRICKY TESTS!

EYE ON THE TARGET!

It's time for your final trial! Each of the words below are hidden somewhere in this grid and it's up to you to find them. Good luck!

ARMOUR
WHIPLASH
WAR MACHINE
BLACK WIDOW
IRON MAN
STARK
REPULSOR
AVENGER
SHIELD
FURY
HARDWARE
JARVIS
INVINCIBLE
SPY

C	S	F	U	R	Y	A	W	D	I	W	B	A
J	E	L	I	N	V	I	N	C	I	B	L	E
N	A	I	W	U	S	G	H	H	O	P	A	W
D	K	R	E	P	U	L	S	O	R	B	C	S
W	X	E	V	W	O	W	A	P	U	V	K	C
A	W	P	K	I	J	S	L	W	E	W	W	N
R	I	S	S	W	S	L	P	W	A	X	I	U
A	Y	W	A	G	W	W	I	W	U	H	D	W
W	W	A	R	M	A	C	H	I	N	E	O	I
P	L	R	W	I	K	O	W	J	R	W	W	R
B	C	M	E	E	W	P	X	E	H	E	W	O
A	J	O	S	A	K	R	I	W	A	W	L	S
V	I	U	W	O	C	E	R	K	R	W	S	T
F	W	R	U	G	S	G	I	W	D	K	J	A
C	S	W	O	J	A	N	U	L	W	O	W	R
O	P	B	E	N	I	E	D	W	A	F	S	K
W	Y	U	K	S	M	V	E	B	R	Q	S	G
S	H	I	E	L	D	A	W	A	E	O	D	W
G	S	P	W	A	N	I	N	U	C	E	W	A

FIND THE ANSWERS ON PAGE 62!

...CONTINUED FROM PAGE 37

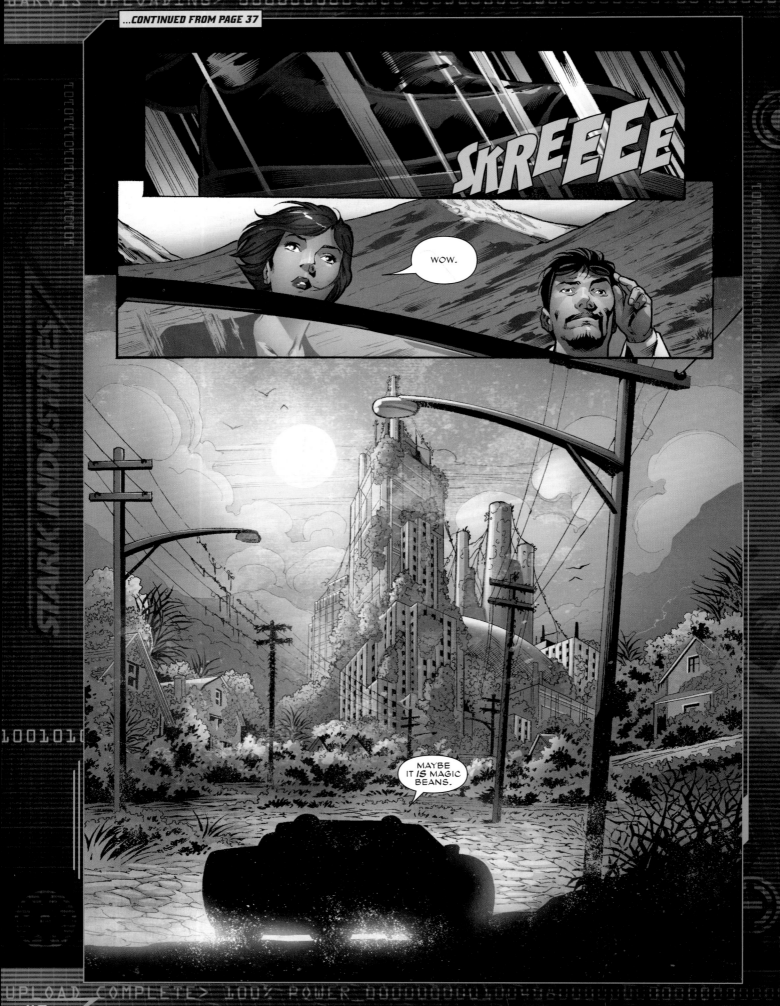

REQUEST VOICE RECOGNITION.

PROCESSING VOICE PATTERN...

IDENTIFIED AS: STARK, TONY.

PASSWORD?

"YINSEN ONE."

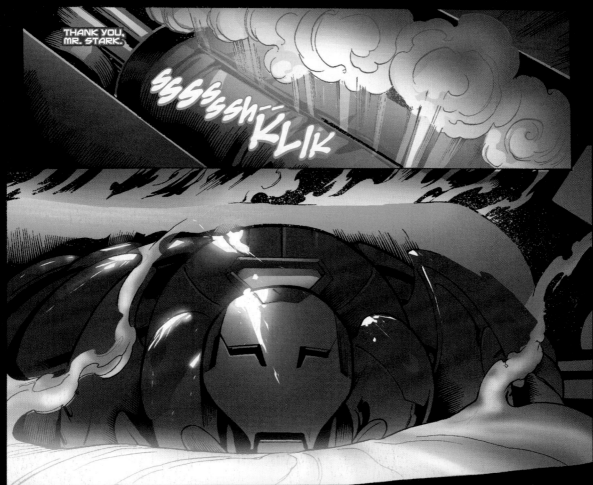

THANK YOU, MR. STARK.

ssssssh--KLIK

CONTINUED ON PAGE 58

WAR MACHINE

BROTHERS IN ARMS

Col. James Rhodes – or Rhodey to his friends – has known Tony Stark since he was a teenager. Even though the two are best buds, the reliable and level headed Rhodey is the complete opposite to his extravagant and carefree friend.

ARMOURED ASSISTANCE!

When the pressure of being Iron Man causes Tony to use the Iron Man armour in increasingly reckless and irresponsible ways, Rhodey comes up with a plan to help him out. He secures the Mark II armour prototype and it is handed over by the military to Justin Hammer to be outfitted with more weapons. Dubbed the 'War Machine' armour, this new suit bristled with hi-tech ordinance, allowing Rhodey to provide the perfect combat support for Iron Man.

WAR MACHINE
TACTICAL ANALYSIS

GE M134 762 M MINI GUN

MISSILE LAUNCHER: KKV SIDEWINDER WITH SECONDARY CYCLOTRIMETHYLENE-TRINITRAMINE RDX BURST

FN2000 BULPUP M-16 WITH M34 MILKOW 40MM GRENADE LAUNCHER

AP9 FULLY AUTOMATIC MACHINE PISTOL

CLARIDGE HITCH 9MM SA PISTOL

C MOVE M24 SHOTGUN WITH IK762 SUPPRESSOR ROUNDS

Ruthless, charming and thoroughly dangerous, Justin Hammer is an unscrupulous businessman and bitter rival of Tony Stark. His company, Hammer Industries, manufactures military weapons and is the United States government's primary defence contractor.

Hammer Industries are desperate to produce their own version of the Iron Man armour, but so far all their prototypes have ended in failure. It seems the only way they will be able to unlock the technology behind the suit is to steal the Iron Man armour from Tony Stark.

LOCATING FILE...
ACCESS CODE: IM1180179
COL. JAMES RHODES/ WAR MACHINE
FILE UNLOCKED... ACCESS GRANTED...

...CONTINUED FROM PAGE 47

UPLOAD COMPLETE> 100% POWER 00000000000010040

BUT WHEN PUSHED, THEY'RE MORE THAN CAPABLE OF DEFENDING THEMSELVES!
FSSSS
FSSSS
WARNING! BOOT TURBINE ONE FAILING! WARNING!
WARNING! BOOT TURBINE TWO FAILING! WARNING!
UH-OH...THOSE FLOWERS SHOT OUT SOME KIND OF ACIDIC ENZYME THAT'S EATING RIGHT THROUGH MY BOOTS!
WARNING! GYRO-STABILIZERS FAILING! COLLISION IMMINENT!
LOSING CONTROL OF--
YOU SEE, MS. POTTS? THE VEGETATIVE WORLD DOES NOT DEFEAT ITS ENEMIES THROUGH VIOLENCE OR DESTRUCTION...
WHOOMPH

YES...THAT'S WHAT HAPPENED... HOW I GOT HERE...

AND NOW...SPORES CLOGGING MY LIMBS... CAN'T MOVE...MANUAL ARMOR RELEASE COMPLETELY GUMMED UP...

THE VINE HAS SEALED OFF THE VENTS... PREVENTED ANY AIR FROM GETTING INSIDE...

AND AS FOR THE ARMOR'S OWN INTERNAL AIR SUPPLY...

BREATHABLE AIR RESERVES AT 0.05% CAPACITY AND DROPPING! WARNING!

...IT'S SPENT. I'M SORRY, PEPPER. I...

I FAILED YOU...JUST LIKE I FAILED PROFESSOR YINSEN. I...

...≫

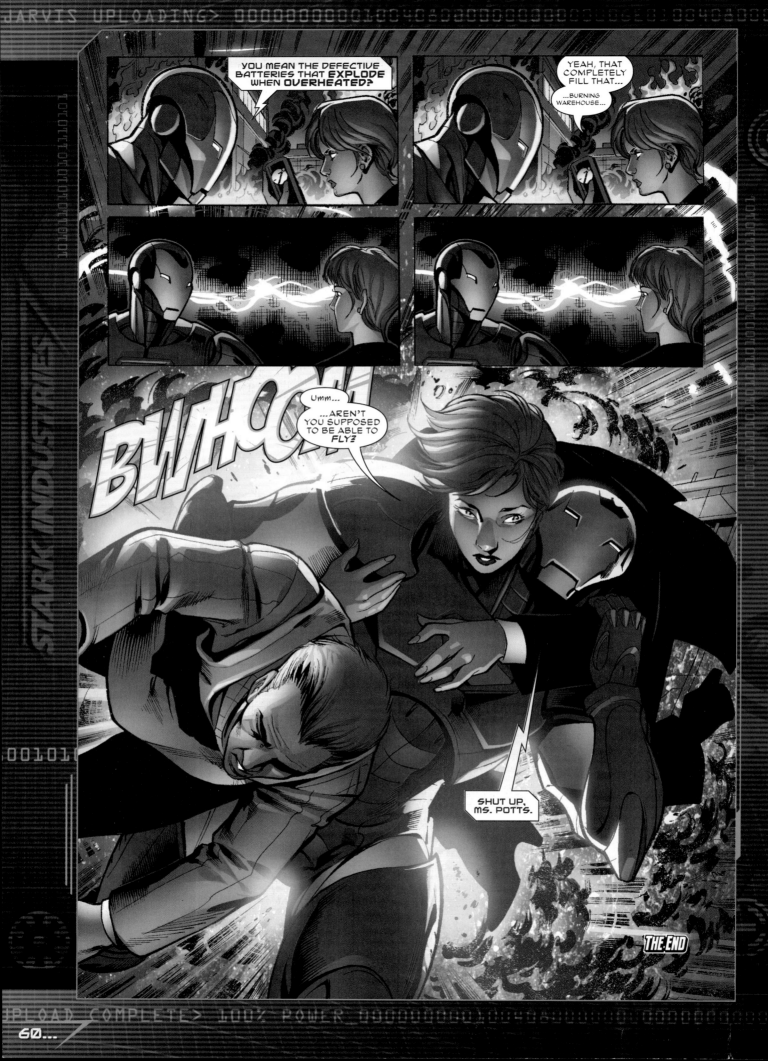

ASSAULT DRONES

Realising that they had a common foe, Justin Hammer broke Ivan Vanko out of jail. He hoped that Vanko would help him design an armoured suit as advanced as Iron Man's.

Hiding him in a secret laboratory, Hammer gave Vanko many unsuccessful prototype suits to experiment on. However, Ivan had his own plans for the armour and instead converted them into a legion of pilotless drones powerful enough to destroy Iron Man!

TACTICAL ASSAULT DRONE

HEIGHT: 210 CM
WEIGHT: 190 KG
ARMAMENTS: AN-M18 Smoke Grenades

SPECIAL FUNCTIONS: Reinforced body armour can withstand high-explosive blasts.

SEA ASSAULT DRONE

HEIGHT: 210 CM
WEIGHT: 220 KG
ARMAMENTS: 16 high-explosive missiles.

SPECIAL FUNCTIONS: Designed for amphibious operations.

GROUND ASSAULT DRONE

HEIGHT: 200 CM
WEIGHT: 230 KG
ARMAMENTS: 120mm smoothbore cannon, 50 Calibre heavy machine gun & XM25 grenade launcher.

SPECIAL FUNCTIONS: Advanced targeting capabilities.

AIR ASSAULT DRONE

HEIGHT: 190 CM
WEIGHT: 150 KG
ARMAMENTS: 4 air-to-air sidewinder missiles.

SPECIAL FUNCTIONS: Thrusters in boots and back allow this unit limited flight capabilities.

ANSWERS

SECRET MISSION...

The hidden Mini-Drones can be found on pages 13, 15, 20, 22, 30, 34, 38, 49 and 57. Entered in the correct order, this should reveal the name of the culprit.

IVAN VANKO

MULTIPLE MENACE!

The answer is **C**.

EYE ON THE TARGET!

```
C S F U R Y A W D I W B A
J E L I N V I N C I B L E
N A I W U S G H H O P A W
D K R E P U L S O R B C S
W X E V W O W A P U V K C
A W P K I J S L W E W W N
R I S S W S L P W A X I U
A Y W A G W W I W U H D W
W W A R M A C H I N E O I
P L R W I K O W J R W W R
B C M E E W P X E H E W O
A J O S A K R I W A W L S
V I U W O C E R K R W S T
F W R U G S G I W D K J A
C S W O J A N U L W O W R
O P B E N I E D W A F S K
W Y U K S M V E B R O S G
S H I E L D A W A E O D W
G S P W A N I N U C E W A
```

START!

ARMS RACE!

31 000
31 BCD
31 20 040 60

FINISH!